107 THINGS I WISH I HAD KNOWN WITH MY FIRST BABY

□

Essential Tips for the First 3 Months

DAWN YANEK

Momsanity Press • New York

First Edition, 2017

ISBN: 978-1-942218-13-5

CONTENTS

ACKNOWLEDGMENTS

A very big thank you to Cara Lynn Shultz and Lynn Messina, my awesome editors and friends who have helped me and motivated me in ways I can't even begin to explain here. Ladies, you rock. To my wonderful, patient husband, Paul: Thank you for all of your support and for building this wonderful little family of ours with me. And finally, the most important thank you of all goes to my two little munchkins—the inspiration for this book and my inspiration to be a better person every day. Mommy loves you both more than anything in the whole world. Also, Mommy is tired. Please go to sleep.

AN INTRODUCTION TO
THE MOMSANITY!

When I was pregnant with my first child, I was nervous but thought, "I've got this." After all, I had nephews, and most of my friends already had kids. I had taken the requisite infant-care and CPR classes. Plus, I'd read plenty of baby books. I knew A LOT.

Hahahaha.

Yeah, no.

Being a first-time mom is quite the learning curve. On my first day home from the hospital with my son, all I could think was: "They let me take this perfect, tiny, breakable, brand-new human home with me. Without a degree. Or a background check. Or any proof of any knowledge whatsoever. What the hell were they thinking? What the hell was *I* thinking?!"

Yes, I had all of that information, a whole lot of love and the sheer determination to get this right. But it was still incredibly hard. I was learning new things about caring for a baby by the minute, and I was struggling to keep up. I assumed this was motherhood.

It was only when I had my second baby last year that I realized that it's not—or, more accurately, that it doesn't have to be.

When my daughter was born, I could not believe how much easier it all was. Yes, *easier*. And it's not because I suddenly had it all together. I was still the same crazy, disorganized, haphazard, messy me that I'd always been. Being a new mom is hard, no matter how many times you do it. All of the usual suspects, like sleep deprivation and postpartum pain, are there and ready to pull you under at any moment. And when you're adding to your brood, there are some new challenges, like how to get your older kid adjusted to life with a sibling. The difference was that all of the day-to-day baby stuff suddenly seemed like common (mom) sense.

When my daughter was just a few weeks old, I decided to share some of that knowledge on my parenting site, Momsanity.com: 15 super practical tips that everyone had forgotten to mention. After I published it, though, I was like, "Oh, wait! Moms need to know how to avoid being covered in spit-up at all times. And that weird thing your nipple does after breastfeeding that shows you that you have a bad latch. Oh, and how could I have forgotten about that magical trick to make a baby close his eyes?!"

So I started jotting down everything I knew but didn't know three and a half years before—about burping, diapering, breastfeeding and more—and I kept writing until my daughter turned 4 months old. No one was more shocked than I was when I realized that I had 107 tips! That's right—107 freaking things that would have made my life a helluva lot easier the first time around and can make *your* life that much easier now.

Of course, it took me nine more months to get around to editing those 107 tips and turning them into this book because I'm a mom of two, my free time is laughable, and, well, that's a whole different issue for a whole different book.

So, expectant and new moms: Don't wait for Baby #2 to do it better. Here's what I wish I had known with my first baby and was so grateful to know the second time around. Happy parenting, and good luck!

Sincerely,

Dawn Yanek, founder of Momsanity.com

CHAPTER 1
DIAPERING

It's a dirty job, but somebody's gotta do it. That would be you…over and over and over again. Babies need up to 10 diaper changes per day, which translates to somewhere between 2,800 and 3,300 diapers for just that first year alone. That sounds terrifying, I know, but after the first few weeks, it won't even faze you. Also terrifying? It's pretty much guaranteed that you'll get peed on and possibly even pooped on at least once. But a few tricks will make diaper changing significantly less crappy—figuratively, if not literally.

Prep for a diaper change before taking off the current dirty diaper. That means opening up the diaper and laying it out next to baby, as well as taking out as many wipes as you think you'll need. (I've gotten it down to a science at three wipes per super poopy newborn diaper.) That way, you won't risk a diaper-free pee while wrangling what you need. Golden showers or worse? No, thanks!

Speaking of that mommy science, here's my cleaning strategy. First, wipe baby's bottom with the diaper itself to get off as much poop as possible. Then, use the first wipe to make sure any remaining poop doesn't get on the changing pad. The second cleans the top and underneath again. The third makes sure that the entire area is indeed poop-free. Of course, this stops working when baby starts eating real food and the poop is more copious, but enjoy the minimal wiping and maximum savings now!

Make sure the diaper ruffle isn't tucked in. Those tiny little frills that circle baby's legs aren't a cutesy decoration—they actually help to prevent leaks.

If baby is having regular poop-splosions and wet onesies, go up a diaper size. Yes, you might still have half a package of tiny diapers left, but make another mom happy and give them to her—and make yourself happy by not having to wash the crib sheets yet again.

It is nearly impossible to make a diaper too tight. A guideline: The sticky fasteners should touch, if not overlap. Anything less and you'll be seeing what's inside that diaper on the outside.

Wrap your dirty diapers into neat little balls. Put dirty wipes inside the dirty diaper, and then securely tape up the whole thing with the fasteners. You might already do this when you're out and about, but it's also a good idea to do when you're at home. You'll avoid getting poop all over your diaper pail, and since the mess is contained, the pail will be less stinky overall.

Don't change your newborn's diaper too soon. Why? Because liquid poop comes in waves. If that's too graphic for you, then you obviously haven't had your baby yet. Anyway, when you're holding baby and you hear and feel the liquid poop (through a diaper), you'll think he's done, because how could your little cherub possibly poop any more, right? Well, he can, and he likely will. Give it a few minutes and then go in.

And speaking of liquid poop, the worst-sounding noises don't always equal the worst poop. That's encouraging, isn't it? Unfortunately, the opposite is also true: Stealthy poops that seem like nothing can actually be a horror show once you unwrap the diaper. When you think about it, diaper changing is a lot like a horror movie: As the unsuspecting protagonist, you should never let your guard down and you should always be prepared for the worst.

When prepping for bath time, don't take off baby's diaper until the last possible second. In other words, don't take it off on the changing table unless you want to get peed on during the walk to the bathroom. It will happen—trust me—and then you'll both need a bath.

You will spend hours talking about poop, examining poop and fretting over what's normal. And chances are, it's all fine! My 9-week-old once went 11 days without pooping, and I was in freak-out mode by Day 3. My pediatrician, however, reassured me that it's common for breastfed babies who are more than 2 months old and haven't started solids yet to go for a while without a bowel movement; they're not even constipated. My kid didn't seem to be bothered by it at all, but after a while, enough was enough (for me). Tummy massages, warm baths, rectal thermometers and prune juice weren't working, so we opted for a doctor-approved baby enema. That did the trick, and we were incredibly relieved.

Enjoy the first four months of poop. Oh, you read that right. While there may be a lot of it, newborn poop is pretty innocuous, especially if you're breastfeeding. It's not as smelly or horrible as you might expect. Once solids are introduced, however, things turn toxic quickly. The poop will also increase in quantity and color, so you'll have a big, old rainbow of it. (Thanks, sweet potatoes and avocados!) In short: It's only going to get worse, so appreciate the cute poop now.

CHAPTER 2
BURPING

What goes in always comes out...and all over you if you're not careful. And that's the least of it. A gassy baby is an uncomfortable baby and, subsequently, a crying baby. These tips will help to soothe baby—and keep the spitting up to a minimum.

Find the sweet spot and stick with it. Over the shoulder has always worked best for me. The shoulder acts as a solid place to compress the gas, as you alternate between firmly patting and rubbing baby's back. It's total personal preference, but this position seems to require the least amount of coordination. Win-win!

Burp your baby even after he's fallen asleep. I know, I know—he's so quiet and peaceful, and you're afraid that burping him now will wake him up. Can't you just quickly put him down? No. He'll likely wake up anyway because he'll spit up as soon as he's flat on his back. The burp will make him feel better, and chances are, it won't wake him up too much—and will actually make him sleep better in the long run.

Stash burp cloths everywhere. Murphy's Law dictates that baby will spit up all over you whenever you've forgotten to grab a burp cloth. Make sure they're strategically placed throughout your house— and in your diaper bag and under the stroller—so that you don't have to go in search of one while you're dripping with puke.

Don't be fooled by cute patterns. By all means, buy the most fashionable burp cloths you can find since they're going to become part of your wardrobe. But beware: Some don't provide enough coverage on your shoulder or lap. Test out a few before committing to buying in bulk. Mark my words: You'll have a favorite.

If baby pulls off your boob or the bottle, burp him now. You might think that his positioning is off and he's uncomfortable. You might think that he just wants to coo and smile at you. You might think that he's full. All of those are possibilities, but more likely, he needs to burp, and if you don't read his mind and do just that, it will be spit-up city.

If you have a particularly bad spitter-upper, protect clothing with a bib. Sometimes babies spit up a while after a feeding, so you're not expecting it. Bibs will also come in handy down the line when teething—and excessive drooling—starts.

Some kids spit up a lot. And some kids don't. I've had one of each, so I can honestly say: It's not me—it's you, kid. I mean, there are ways to minimize the spitting up—by not overfeeding, by slowing things down and by burping regularly—but a lot of it simply boils down to how mature a child's digestive system is or isn't. In short, sometimes spit-up happens, no matter what preventive measures you take.

CHAPTER 3
BREASTFEEDING
AND ASSORTED BOOB ISSUES

How to feed your baby is arguably the most volatile subject in a new mom's life. Everyone has an opinion, and those opinions aren't always helpful or kind. So let me put this out there right away: Fed is best. Whether you choose to breastfeed, exclusively pump, use formula or do some combination of the above, it's all good. As long as your baby is happy, healthy and gaining weight, do whatever works best for you and is right for your family.

That said, if you choose to breastfeed, it might feel anything but natural in those first few weeks. But once you get the hang of it and your body gets used to the idea of a little creature attaching itself to your boobs, it can be an awesome—and eventually, a surprisingly easy—experience. If you're interested in breastfeeding and have time to read only one section of this book right now, this should be it.

If nursing hurts and doesn't get better within 10 seconds, unlatch and try, try again. When I was a brand-new mom, I was terrified to unlatch my son. I was just so happy that he was eating, and I thought that if I took him off my breast, he'd never latch on again. Yeah, no chance of that happening. Babies are hungry and persistent, so unlatch, relatch and repeat as many times as necessary. Your hungry little barracuda might get a tiny bit irritated with you, but he'll learn the right way to feed—and fast.

But on the flip side, don't stress about mastering all the ways to latch a baby onto your boob. If you've got a position that works for you, stick with it. With my son, I worried that I had only one good option in my breastfeeding arsenal for each side, and that one wasn't "optimal," according to the lactation consultants. But hey, it worked, my boobs weren't raw, and neither of my babies ever complained. The takeaway? Expert advice is great...up to a point.

In the early days, there's nothing delicate about latching a baby on your boob. This completely surprised me in the hospital. When the nurses and lactation consultants were helping me to get the hang of things, they would practically shove my kid onto my boob so that he opened his mouth wide enough. So support baby's neck, get him to open his mouth properly by aligning your nipple with the top of his nose (not the middle of his mouth), hold your breast and put as much of that breast as possible in his mouth.

When the books talk about a lazy latch, they're talking about a nipple-only latch. And it hurts. Baby's mouth needs to open a lot wider for effective nursing that doesn't hurt like a mother. In fact, I'm pretty sure that "open wider" was the first thing my days-old daughter understood. Funny enough, though, this changes over time. By the time she was 5 months old, she could do a much more shallow latch without having it hurt at all.

If your baby seems insatiable, that's because he is. He's likely cluster feeding—i.e., nursing all the time with barely a break between sessions—because he's going through a growth spurt. This generally happens at night, and it's exhausting. The good news? Your baby will sleep *a lot* the day after a milk marathon, and your uterus will contract more, making your postpartum bump go down a little faster.

Invest in a sleep bra for nursing. Even though it's normally lovely for the girls to be free at night—Lord knows this was the case while you were pregnant—the polar opposite can be true when you've got what feels like a gallon of milk weighing down each boob. This gets better once your body regulates your milk supply, but in the beginning and especially with your first baby, it can be really uncomfortable; for me, it was downright painful. A sleep bra is basically a stretchy, crisscross bra that doesn't have clips at the straps like a regular nursing bra. It gives you the support you need while also allowing for super easy access when you're half-asleep.

Put nursing pads in that sleep bra so you don't leak through your pajama top. If your newborn is— God willing—sleeping for more than two hours at a stretch, you will have two wet bull's-eyes reminding you of that in the morning, at least early on. (See above.) One time, milk actually splashed through my shirt and onto my arm, and my 3-year-old asked me what in the hell it was...though in a much more age-appropriate way. Nursing pads are also great if you're using lanolin to soothe your chomped-on boobs: While wonderful, that stuff is oily and can stain clothing.

Speaking of lanolin, stock up. It's like Vaseline...but with magical properties. Apply it after you've finished a nursing session to soothe your poor nipples when they're off duty. While it's safe to use while breastfeeding, I still always liked to wipe my breasts with a damp washcloth if I had one handy so that my baby didn't ingest it. And in case you're wondering, this wasn't an issue when I needed to feed baby in public. By the time I was ready to be out in public and nursing, my boobs were pretty much healed, and I no longer needed the lanolin.

If you have a marathon feeder, detach him from your breast after 15 to 20 minutes. My son would have been attached to me 24/7 if I let him—and I did let him for the first few weeks. I'm pretty sure he was on each side for 40 minutes a pop. As a first-time mom, I thought he was constantly starving, and I was desperate to make sure he was getting enough food. But after 20 minutes, there's no more milk left in that breast (or, more accurately, very little). Move baby onto the other side, or change activities if he's full.

Just because a baby is latched, it doesn't mean he's eating. Being a baby is exhausting, and being with Mommy is oh-so-comforting. It's incredibly easy for your little one to fall asleep on the breast and/or to use it as a makeshift pacifier. You can tell if baby is actually eating by looking at his jawbone and his ear. If they're moving up and down, he's eating. If they're not, then he's not.

And just to reiterate, your boobs are *not* pacifiers.
Unless baby is sick, has just had his shots or needs to
be soothed to sleep after you've been up for way too
many hours. Then all bets are off. Otherwise, for the
sake of your poor, red, sore boobs, nip this habit in
the bud, so to speak.

**Your bigger boob doesn't necessarily produce
more milk.** I haven't taken a formal poll, but from
what I understand, most women have two different-
sized breasts. My left one is significantly bigger than
my right, so it seemed logical to me that it would
produce more milk. Nope! I was shocked to find that
it actually produced significantly less when I pumped.
A fun bit of knowledge to have for parties (or not),
but more important, it gave me a sense of how long
my little one wanted to feed on each side and how
soon he needed to be burped.

When you get the hang of it, nursing will tickle.
Good news: Your nipples won't always feel like
they've been doused with battery acid. Breastfeeding
can actually be pleasant, and you can have those sweet

moments you've imagined all along. That's my way of saying: Hang in there if you want to! As long as there aren't any issues like a tongue tie or low supply, it gets better; it really does.

Babies' tummies are tiny. Every breastfeeding new mom on the planet worries that she's starving her child. But this information from the La Leche League should calm your fears: On Day 1, baby's stomach capacity is the size of a marble—really, that's it!—and by Day 7, it's about the size of a ping-pong ball. Wet diapers and consistent weight gain (after the initial loss right after birth) are signs that all is working as it should, but *always* talk to your doctor if you're even slightly concerned.

Feel yourself up to figure out which side is due for breastfeeding. In the hospital and for the first few days, when you're not sure how much you're producing and both boobs hurt for a variety of reasons, you'll want to keep track of which side you fed on last. Try writing it down or plugging the info into an app. But soon, you can just cop a quick feel and get your answer. I'm not going to lie—it's a lot like feeling melons at the grocery store. "Hmmm…this one feels a little soft. This one is round and full." Weird but effective!

The shape of your nipple after nursing can tell you a lot. If it's round and, well, nipple-like right when it comes out of baby's mouth, you're golden. If it's flat or somehow squished, the latch is off—which you most likely know already since you're probably in pain.

If baby falls asleep while nursing, move him ever-so-slightly to wake him up. That's really all you need to do. No foot tickles, no face caresses and the like, as the books recommend. That did nothing except make my kids snuggle more— which, admittedly, was cute, but didn't achieve the desired effect. Instead, a lactation consultant I spoke to after having my second child advised me to tilt baby's head back a tiny bit to make the sucking reflex kick in again. And you know what? It does. Instantly.

An FYI: It is so damn hard to stay awake while breastfeeding. It's a combination of the cuddle hormone oxytocin released during nursing and sheer exhaustion, but it was nearly impossible for me to keep my eyes open, especially in the middle of the night. Make sure you're nursing in a safe spot, and try to have your significant other check on you periodically so you can put the baby down in his crib and everyone can get some proper sleep.

Introduce a bottle early. I navigated this challenge well the first time around, but only accidentally. My son's sugar was low, so the doctors suggested supplementing a teensy-tinsy bit with formula in the hospital. After that, he easily switched between boob and bottle. I realize that giving the occasional bottle of formula to a nursing baby so early on is controversial, but it worked for us: My boobs got the occasional break, my husband got to be involved in some of the feedings, and there was absolutely no nipple confusion. Fast-forward to baby #2, when breastfeeding was a lot easier and when I didn't have a chance to pump or buy formula because I was so busy trying to deal with two kids. Well, when I attempted to give my daughter a bottle—I tried pumped milk and formula—around Week 8, she rejected it. With gusto. We didn't have any success with a bottle until Week 22.

Fed is best. I mentioned this in the introduction to this section, but it's worth repeating. It's something I've always believed, but in those early days of motherhood and attempted breastfeeding, I still felt a little guilty about giving him formula every now and then. In retrospect, this was CRAZY. Breastmilk, formula—it doesn't matter. As long as your baby is eating and thriving, it's all good. Everyone is different, but for me, the occasional bottle took the pressure off a little, helped me through the challenging times and strengthened my desire to breastfeed. My cracked nipples healed, my son and I got into a nursing groove, and breastfeeding became an overwhelmingly positive experience for both of us.

CHAPTER 4
BABY CLOTHES

They're tiny! They're cute! They're everywhere! You may feel like you're drowning in a sea of little outfits in need of constant laundering...probably because you are. Here's how you can manage all of your adorable little one's adorable little things without losing your mind.

Don't overdress or underdress baby. New moms tend to overdress their newborns (they're tiny and they're freezing!), while new dads tend to underdress them (they're little heat machines and they're sweating!). Here's a good rule of thumb: Dress baby in one layer more than you're comfortable wearing that day. And remember that if it's ninth-circle-of-hell hot, it'll be hot for everyone—baby included.

The hospital will probably be the only place you'll use newborn hats. Of course I'm not talking about the hats that baby will need outside on cold days. I'm talking about those cute, coordinated, lightweight hats. Sometimes they'll come with an outfit, and honestly, a few are all you'll need. If it's cool out, you might use one, but most jackets will have a hood so it becomes redundant. And indoors, baby's head will be fine without it. In fact, studies have shown that skin-to-skin contact with you is the thing that actually regulates baby's body temperature. So skip the hat. Chances are, you'll lose it somewhere anyway.

You need newborn clothing. Every book and nearly everyone will tell you that it's a waste of money, but trust me when I say that you'll need and want at least a few items. Why? Babies are tiny! Even clothes in 0 to 3 months will swim on most newborns. My son was 8 pounds 13 ounces at birth, and I still had him in newborn clothing for a few weeks. Sure, your baby will grow into that bigger size relatively quickly, but think about it: You will take the most pictures of your baby in the first month of his life. Need I say more?

Aside from buying a few newborn pieces, step away from the clothing that fits 6 months and younger. Those tiny outfits are impossible to resist, but do your best to limit your purchases. Why? You'll be getting loads of clothing in those sizes from family and friends. Instead, save your money for 9 months and older. People rarely buy gifts in those sizes—and you'll want to give a big, sloppy kiss to those who do when baby outgrows his current size and you suddenly have nothing that fits. After that, you'll be dipping into your own wallet a lot more often and a lot more deeply.

Don't buy too much too far in advance. This is something that I learned only recently, and it really depends on your kid. My son was always off-the-charts big (and still is). My daughter, on the other hand, is on the smaller end of the spectrum. I would have had her in the wrong size all winter if I had gone by what I thought she'd be wearing by then.

If you don't know about flash-sale sites like Zulily and Rue La La, let me introduce you to

your new BFFs. Sales are the way to go with as many things as possible since baby will be in the next size before you know it. Also, very little in life beats the adrenaline rush of getting an awesome deal...especially when you don't even have to leave your house to get it. Warning: This can be as dangerous to your wallet as it sounds.

Hand-me-downs are even better than you think. It's fun to see something on your baby that was once worn by a good friend's child, but it also can potentially save you a fortune. Items like swimsuits and snowsuits, which don't give you a lot of bang for your buck unless you live near a beach or in a particularly cold area, are especially great. Use what you can; pass along the rest to someone else.

You don't have to use the very specific brand of baby detergent you've been told to use. Without naming names, there is one brand that corners this market. As a first-time mom, I didn't want to make any mistakes and desperately wanted to protect my baby's sensitive skin. The thing is, it made me sneeze, so it wasn't fragrance-free like I thought it would be. Still, I stubbornly washed and rewashed my baby's clothes in it for weeks, maybe months…until I came to my senses. Anything "free and clear"—i.e., fragrance-free and gentle—will do the trick.

Newborn socks will be the bane of your existence. Invest in onesies with footies, especially for nighttime, as well as in Sock Ons, which stretch over those pesky socks and keep them in place.

Your baby doesn't need shoes…but you'll still really want to buy them. Those precious little toes curl adorably, which makes it next to impossible to keep shoes on them. There's a reason why so many socks are made to look like Mary Janes and sneakers. Stock up on those, and then buy one pair of ridiculously cute, soft-soled shoes on sale if you really can't help yourself. You might put them on baby only once, but the photo op will be worth it.

Invest in baby mittens. Until those oddly soft yet sharp nails firm up and you can trim them, you'll want to play defense and keep them away from baby's precious face when he fusses and fidgets. Why mittens don't come with every infant onesie, like those little hats, is beyond me. And oddly, they're not that easy to find. My favorite were from Giggle, which my husband discovered after our week-old son ended up with itty-bitty, very red scratches all over his face after a nap. You'll also want to look for newborn onesies that have extra fabric at the wrists that can be folded over those little talons.

Onesies with buttons were created by the Devil.
Yes, the actual Devil. Clothing with buttons is usually particularly adorable and you'll think you can handle it. For special occasions, you can. But for everyday situations—like when baby is screaming because he has a poopy diaper, or there's a judgey relative nearby and your fingers are shaking and sweaty from the pressure of being watched—you'll want to do things as swiftly and as easily as possible. So go with the snaps or a zipper and make at least one thing easier on yourself.

CHAPTER 5
SLEEPING

Sleep—or lack thereof—is one of the most stressful parts of becoming a parent. We research it, we meticulously schedule nap times and bedtimes, we obsess...and our best-laid plans still usually fall apart. Now listen to my next sentence. No, really listen to it: *This is normal.* Babies are trying to get used to life outside your warm, cozy belly, and they want to be held. Their tummies are tiny, and they want to eat frequently. In short: They're babies, and you just have to go with the flow. And now for the next part that you also need to hear: It *will* get better. I promise. Here are a few ways to lay the groundwork now and make that happen over the next few months.

Read all the books on sleep training, and then pick and choose which bits to use. Caveat: unless you're choosing one particular method that involves a specific schedule…and you like it…and it works for you. The thing is, if there was one perfect way to get a baby to sleep, then there would be only one book out there. Do what you're comfortable with, and that's what will be best for you and your family.

Set up a separate nighttime area for yourself before going to bed. You and your baby will not be sleeping through the night in the beginning. It's a biological fact: Newborns need to eat every few hours. You might want to feed in the comfort of your own bed, but this never worked for me. I was a lot more comfortable on the living room couch, as long as it was set up the way I liked it: nursing pillow, burp cloth, bottle of water to keep me hydrated (which I really needed since I was nursing), pillows propped up just so and a blanket in case I was chilly. Make sure you're set up before bedtime, so when baby wakes, you're good to go and it'll be much easier to go back to bed when you're done.

Swaddle well and swaddle early. For the first two months of my son's life, I was convinced that he didn't like to be swaddled. And maybe he didn't, but only because I was doing it wrong—i.e., wrapping him too loosely. Because of that, he was frustrated, pulled a Houdini every night and escaped from his baby straitjacket. Once I honed my baby-burrito wrapping skills, we all slept much better. Everyone loves a different wrap—from the ubiquitous Aden + Anais blanket (which is also great as a lightweight stroller blanket and a nursing cover) to a slightly thicker yet still soft one from Swaddle Designs, which was my go-to the first time around. With my second baby, however, I was obsessed with the easy-to-wrap Summer Infant swaddle and its Velcro fastener. Seriously, why make more work for yourself?

But a quick safety note about swaddling... Never put baby on his stomach when swaddled (or at all when you put him down), and stop using the swaddle once he's able to roll over.

You don't need to get baby out of his swaddle for a nighttime feeding. I learned this the hard way with my son...and honestly, I didn't figure it out until I had my daughter. I thought that he would want his hands free to be comfortable while eating (he didn't) and that I'd need to check his diaper for poop, just in case (you can smell it through the swaddle if it's there). Taking him out of the swaddle only woke him up further, and it woke him up even more when I had to reswaddle him. At that point, he was up and thought it was time to party.

Sleeping through the night means a very different thing to babies than it does to us. If you're thinking that it means a 12-hour stretch in the first three months, let me stop you right there. At this stage of the game, sleeping through the night usually means six hours. Max. Enjoy those nights when you get them.

If baby is having a great time and then he's suddenly not, he's tired. Being a baby is exhausting! Moods can literally turn on a dime. Think of it as preparation for when you have a threenager. (And no, I didn't mean teenager. Just wait till you get to age 3 and your child suddenly has OPINIONS.) If burping doesn't help, it's time for snuggles, swaddles and sleep.

When baby is visibly tired and super cranky, you've waited too long. And when you've waited too long, you'll have a harder time getting him to settle down and sleep well. Instead, look for early cues such as that first eye rub or sudden calmness and quiet. Parents often mistake that quiet for actual peace and quiet...but it's not. It's the beginning of the end, so get that baby to bed quickly!

Skip the padded crib bumpers. I couldn't help but buy one for my son because it was so cute and it really completed the room. But the American Academy of Pediatrics has officially come out against the use of crib bumpers because they can add to the risk of SIDS. After stressing out every time I put my son in his crib and checking him obsessively because I was worried he'd suffocate on the damn thing, I threw it out.

Mesh bumpers are a godsend. They're not particularly pretty—and they may even remind you of a bad '80s shirt (um, just me?)—but they do the job. What job? Making sure that your baby doesn't get his limbs stuck in the crib's slats or that a pacifier doesn't fall to the floor...behind the crib...impossible to get to without moving the entire stupid thing...which you really don't want to do at 3 a.m....unless you're completely desperate...which is usually the case.

Bedtime routines are magical. In the first few weeks, don't bother—you're in survival mode. But around the third or fourth week, when things are starting to settle down a little, try experimenting with a nighttime routine: a darkened room, a (wishful) last feeding, a few books, a softly sung song or two. While it will take some time for baby to get with the program, he will eventually pick up on the idea that sleepy time is on its way.

Close your eyes to make baby close his. Before my son was born, one of my friends warned: When he's trying to fall asleep, do not make eye contact! I thought she was overreacting. She wasn't. Do it and baby's eyes will pop open like one of those old-fashioned dolls. Instead, exhibit sleepy behavior and baby will mimic you. *You're feeling sleepy, very sleepy....*

Make sure baby's room is pitch-black. If you don't have blackout curtains and if you haven't taped up the sides of the windows to make sure that light isn't creeping in, it's not dark enough.

When you're gently putting baby down in his crib, don't drop and run. I know, this seems like common sense, but hear me out. I was terrified that if my daughter felt my hand on her, she would wake up and start crying immediately. In fact, the exact opposite was true. The abruptness of laying her down in her crib was too jarring; she suddenly felt alone and unsnuggled. Instead, it worked better to keep my hands on her for a few seconds while she settled into the crib and adjusted to a cool mattress and a less snuggly sleeping situation, and then gently remove those hands and inch backward out the door.

All of your hard work might go out the window at 4 months. If this is the first time you're hearing about the 4-month sleep regression, I am sorry to be the bearer of bad news. It doesn't happen with every kid, but it happens more often than not, from what I understand, AND NO ONE TALKS ABOUT IT BEFORE IT HAPPENS. From the all caps right there, you can likely surmise that I think people should talk about it. So there's my big, fat warning to you! The good news is that it will eventually even out...but then you'll be smacked with teething and developmental spurts, both of which can disrupt sleep.

Remember that newborns sleep a lot. Granted, they're up at weird hours and sometimes it's all the time, but seriously, they will never sleep this much again. If you can figure out how to roll with the weirdness of it all, you can actually get a lot done during the naps. Or, you know, just stare at the perfection you've created—or the wall, depending on how tired you are.

What you do in the first three months won't affect how your child sleeps forever. Really. A mom can make herself crazy by worrying about how every little thing she does now will negatively impact her child for the rest of his life. But there is no relation to how your newborn sleeps (or, more to the point, doesn't sleep) right now and how he'll sleep months and years from now. Try to remember that in these first few weeks, it's all about comfort and survival—for both of you.

Overall, do what works for you. For me, this meant that during baby's naps, my daughter was usually snuggling in my arms. Instead of binge-watching *Pretty Little Liars* (again), I tried to get a little Momsanity writing done, so I devised a solution with her on my chest, the Boppy on my lap and the computer perched on the Boppy. The thing is, I knew she wouldn't be sleeping on me forever (or even past the 3- or 4-month mark). This little girl was my last baby, and I wanted to enjoy every minute of her and every minute of those early days together. That said, when I needed to use the bathroom, fold some laundry or just stretch my aching back, baby went into the bouncy seat. And at night, she spent as much time as possible in the bassinet next to my bed, because I also wanted to get her used to sleeping without me. Just not too far away from me—or all the time without me right away.

CHAPTER 6
BABY MAINTENANCE

Here are a few things to remember about those confounding little bundles of joy. Also, wondering what that smell is? Read on for a few likely culprits!

Baby's hair can fall out. And my son's did. It happened somewhere during the second and third week, and he looked like a little old, half-bald man. It took a year to grow back, but now, four years later, he has an uncontrollable, thick mess of hair. So try not to freak out too much. It will grow...eventually.

Use one of your nail files on baby's nails. The thought of attempting to clip baby's soft, bendy, practically transparent nails—and the possibility of accidentally clipping that delicate skin—made me want to vomit. And baby nail files just don't do the trick. Seriously, I'd be filing away at my newborn's nails forever, and I'm sure you can imagine how that went with a squirmy, irritated infant who refused to sleep during this delightful event. I even tried some sort of spinning gadget that was supposed to gently get rid of rough edges. Totally ineffective as well. It was only with my second baby that I broke out my own cardboard nail file from Revlon. Success! It's safe, and it gets the job done fast.

Boogie Wipes may be the best invention ever for runny noses. But, you say, can't you just use a tissue or a regular wipe? No. Tissues, no matter how soft and coated with aloe, are too rough for baby's delicate skin. And wipes can leave residue on baby's face and sting a raw nose. But Boogie Wipes are a godsend: Their saline softens up crusty snot (lovely, I know, but that's our reality), and they're übergentle. Stock up on these—seriously, never have less than three packs in your possession at all times—because you never know when the stores will run out or when a cold will strike.

Move baby's bouncy seat from room to room, as needed. If you don't have one, invest in one ASAP. It would be great if baby would contentedly coo and cuddle wherever you put him, wouldn't it? Yeah, that's not going to happen. Baby will want to see you and have you rock him and sing to him, but aside from that, you'll want to keep an eye on him as you're making food or getting ready for the day. That ginormous swing might be great, but if you can't pick it up and fit it in a small space, it's not enough.

If your kid worships at the altar of the binky, buy a pacifier clip. Such a simple concept, you'll be annoyed that someone thought of it before you did and probably made a gazillion dollars. One end loops around the pacifier ring, while the other clips to your baby's shirt. Voilà! No more pacifiers dropped onto dirty, germy supermarket floors…until your kid figures out how to unclip the clip. (I think we made it to 18 months.)

Beware of your hair. A single strand of your hair can get wrapped around a baby's finger or toe. It's called a hair tourniquet, and it can be super dangerous. My son was obsessed with my hair, and it's a true miracle that this never happened to him—especially since I wasn't even aware that it *could* happen. But recently, it's been in the news, and it actually happened to a friend of mine and her baby. The issue is that it can get wrapped around so tightly, it starts to cut off the blood supply to a finger or toe. Some signs that it might be happening: uncontrollable crying for seemingly no reason, and a digit that's very red and swollen. Blond moms may be at more risk since their hair is so light, but it can happen with anyone.

Baby boners are a thing. Yes, I just wrote that down. I know it sounds so basic, but as a woman, this never occurred to me. When I was changing my son's diaper in the first week or two after he was born, I saw something...strange. I called/yelled for my husband to come into the room. He tried not to laugh as he assured me that everything was not only fine but also better than fine because it meant that the baby's plumbing was working correctly. Yeah, so that happened.

The umbilical cord can stick around for longer than you think. And you'll likely Google pictures of gooey, infected umbilical cords to make sure that your baby's is A-OK. To help the healing process, get diapers with a special umbilical cord cutout or fold down the top of the diaper until the little stump falls off so it doesn't irritate the area.

Babies can smell fear. It sounds like the tagline to a horror movie, and at 3 a.m., when you haven't slept for more than two hours straight for more days than you can count, it feels like you're living in one. It boils down to this: So much of getting your baby to calm down is about your energy. Even if you think you're exhibiting calm, you might not be. I remember singing sweetly and quietly to my son with no luck. I thought I was calm, but when I took a deep breath and relaxed my arms, I realized that I hadn't been. And you know what? The second I did that and maintained that vibe, he mirrored my energy in his little body, relaxed into my arms and (eventually, mercifully) closed his eyes.

Sunscreen isn't safe for babies younger than 6 months old. That's right—even baby sunscreen. Who knew?! Not me, until I double-checked with my doctor after reading the fine print on the sunscreen bottle. The key here is to be smart. If you're going to the beach or the park, avoid the strongest sunlight in the middle of the day, and instead, go out before 10 a.m. or after 4 p.m. And while there, keep baby covered with a hat, clothing with a UPF number (basically an SPF rating system for clothes), and a protective baby tent or a good, old-fashioned shady tree.

Sock lint smells rancid. There's nothing better than kissing those soft, little baby feet…except when they smell like something unholy. For the longest time, I couldn't figure out what was going on with my son. I bathed him regularly, but we still had this problem. I finally realized that the tiniest bit of lint can hide between the folds of those tiny toes and stay there. Trust me: Don't miss these spots.

Always keep one hand on baby while he's on the changing table, even if you don't have a squirmer. I actually knew this before my son arrived because I'd heard terrifying stories about falls. Still, it's worth mentioning here. It seems so unlikely that they'll roll off in those first few weeks, but it *can* happen in that half a second that you lean over to throw out a diaper or bend down to get an outfit out of a drawer. Don't make the mistake of thinking that it won't happen to you.

Spit-up can pool behind the ears. If you're wondering where in the hell the smell is coming from when you hug your sweet baby, it's here. My son was a spitter-upper, and even though I would obviously clean him each and every time he spit up, remnants of it got in that little fold right behind his ear. Soap and water will do the trick, but a quick wipe with a burp cloth won't.

To the (potentially germy) children who want to touch your baby: Clothes and toes only! I learned this phrase from a fellow mom after I had my second child, and it has been incredibly helpful when dealing with toddlers and preschoolers who just loooove tiny babies. I wish I'd had this language when my son was born because what came out of my mouth instead was a panicked: "Oh, sweetie, please don't touch the baby!!!" Of course, the kids in question would just keep trying to touch the baby because they're kids. The "clothes and toes" directive, however, is something they can remember and abide by…at least until you can pick up baby and get him out of the way of those grabby hands.

You can't spoil a baby. Chances are, if you've heard this phrase, you've also heard that you can, indeed, spoil a baby. Trust me when I say that you can't, so feel free to tell the little old bitty who insists that babies can be spoiled to shut it. Babies are not manipulative. They will not become brats if you pick them up, hold them and generally tend to their needs. They are babies! If they are crying, they need something specific, even if it's only to be held. Remember: There is no "only" when it comes to a baby. Whatever small thing you're doing for them is everything to them at that moment.

CHAPTER 7
MOMMY MAINTENANCE

Caring for a newborn is a full-time, overwhelming, insane job. It's easy to put your own health and well-being on the back burner. But—and I know that we all know this somewhere in those frazzled, sleep-deprived brains of ours—that doesn't help anyone in the long run. We have needs, too. No one is saying that you should book a spa day when you've got a 2-week-old, but even the most minimal self-care can make the transition into motherhood a lot easier. With that in mind, here's what you can expect in the days after D day.

Take that shower. This will seem like an impossible dream in a few short weeks, but right now—in the early days of new mommyhood when your significant other and various helpful elves are around—do it. Your poor, beat-up body will feel exponentially better, and your brain will be a lot less fuzzy.

Don't give up the sitz bath, squeezy bottle and pain meds too early. You might feel miraculously better some days, but that's the surest way to make sure that you suddenly don't. If you've had a vaginal birth, you've had some major trauma down below and maybe some stitches; things need tending to. And, of course, self-care is extra important if you've had a C-section. Even minimal maintenance will help you take care of baby a helluva lot better.

Lock the damn door—to use the bathroom or to take a nap. Your significant other and baby will both be OK, even if you hear slight crying from one and/or both of them. In fact, they'll be more than OK, because they'll forge their own bond and learn to work out these mini-problems without you.

You will likely wake up every night for weeks drenched in sweat. Ah, night sweats. Why did no one tell me about those? It's a combination of hormones and sweating out the water weight, and while you'll be thrilled to be less swollen the next day...holy hell, you'll also be soaked and shivering. This could last a few weeks, and you'll never be so happy to get in the shower afterward. (See above about taking advantage of those showers in the early days!) And did I mention the sweating-off-the-weight part?

There will be blood. Oh, so much blood. Remember the elevator scene in *The Shining*? Yeah, it's like that. Everyone's body is different, but in those first few days after childbirth, things aren't pretty. After I had my first child, I experienced pretty intense bleeding for more than four months, which certainly didn't feel normal—but apparently happens sometimes, according to my doctors. (If this is happening to you, by the way, it's essential that you get checked out like I did.) The good news? It was completely different with my second. The majority of the bleeding slowed and almost stopped after two to three weeks.

Stay hydrated. Constipation can become a real issue in the days and weeks after childbirth, similar to when you first got pregnant. And this can be extra miserable if you have hemorrhoids from labor. Here's the thing I didn't realize: If you're breastfeeding, the water level in your body can get depleted even more. And even if you're not, pain medication can also do the same thing in those early days. Keep water nearby at all times—and also take the stool softener that the doctors likely recommended in the hospital—to stay ahead of this issue.

Buy two nursing bras before baby is born—and only two. It's a pain to have to go out and buy more when you're bleary-eyed and barely leaving the house, but your boobs will change and might grow yet again (yes, seriously), so you might size yourself out of your current bra. The nursing-bra specialists I worked with recommended waiting three to four weeks to buy more, once your breasts have settled—and once you're semi-settled in.

That belly stripe isn't going away anytime soon. Pregnancy leaves its mark on your body well beyond the baby weight. I didn't particularly want to get into a bikini anytime soon, but I was kind of hoping that weird line—technically called the linea nigra—would magically disappear once I gave birth. Nope! Much to my surprise, it stayed put until after I stopped breastfeeding (though it did get lighter). Hormones are fun, aren't they?

Don't get your rings resized just yet. Much like the belly line, I thought that my fingers would go back to normal shortly after giving birth. I mean, the insane bloating was gone and the weight was already starting to come off. But, no, the fingers were still swollen. Some women report issues from a few weeks to up to a year, and some eventually break down and go for the resizing. With my son, I was back in my rings at 4 months. With my daughter, I finally got back in them at 11 months.

Your hair can fall out. Somewhere between three and six months after giving birth to my first child, a big clump of hair on the left side of my hairline fell out...and grew back gray. Fun! (You did get the sarcasm in that, right? Just checking.) According to science, this is because pregnancy hormones keep a normal amount of hair from falling out on a daily basis. But when those hormones calm the eff down, that hair starts to shed. So, that sucks, but at least you can console yourself with the knowledge that you're just losing the hair that should have come out while pregnant. As for the gray hair? I haven't gotten any good answers for that one—and I haven't found any way to feel better about it either. I might just be old, but I think it's more like when the mom in *Poltergeist* ended up with a gray streak after rescuing Carol Ann from the other side. Ghosts, new babies—equally traumatic! Anyway, the good news is that neither of those things happened with my second baby.

Your back might hurt. And it might hurt oh-so-much, which says something since you've already been through the back pain of pregnancy. Maybe I was a little more out of shape the second time around, but I seriously had to rely on my stroller for support when walking down the street. My core was shot, and my poor back was overcompensating to keep me upright. Plus, I was falling asleep in the most uncomfortable positions with baby. Stretching and yoga-style exercises really helped.

There is such a thing as postpartum anxiety. Everyone talks about postpartum depression, and I didn't have that. I was so happy and so grateful that my son was here and healthy, I felt like my heart was going to burst. And then I felt like I couldn't breathe—and I certainly couldn't sleep—because I was worried that something would happen to him. And I was worried *all the time.* The anxiety dreams woke me up every hour when my son didn't, and I devised "What would you do?" baby-crisis scenarios in my head constantly. This was not normal, and I had no idea until I was pregnant with my second child. If you experience anything similar, talk to a friend or a professional, or at least know that you are not crazy.

You will have cramps *after* you give birth. Your uterus is going down to its normal size, and soon, you might actually not look like you're still pregnant. On the flip side, for the first few days after childbirth, this might hurt. A lot.

If you've had an episiotomy, it'll get worse before it gets better. The healing pain after my episiotomy almost sent me to the hospital because I thought I'd popped my stitches or that something was seriously wrong. Think about it this way: You know how when a wound heals, you get a scab, and it kind of tugs on either side of your skin as it heals? That's what's happening down below. The stitches pull as your body knits itself back together, especially if you're exerting yourself more than you should, and it can be really...unpleasant. I imagine the same would be more than true for C-section stitches as well, so, mamas, take it as easy as you can until you are fully healed!

When you have that first glass of wine, it will hit you—hard. You haven't had anything to drink in 10 months, maybe more, and your tolerance is pretty much what it was the first day of your freshman year.

Ask for help. Full disclosure: I was awful at this. I didn't ask my husband nearly enough to take the baby so I could sleep. I didn't ask my mom to empty the dishwasher. I didn't ask my friends to bring food when I really could have used it. I am an idiot. Granted, this is part of a larger personality issue—I'm always worried about inconveniencing people—and I am trying to get it under control, which is a whole other story. But I had to put my insecurities and my pride aside when I had my second baby because I just couldn't do it all. Plus, I was motivated by a desire to make the sibling transition as easy as possible for my older child. It was only then that I realized how much easier my life would have been if I had mastered the art of asking the first time around. The other thing? People *want* to help because they love you. Let them.

Involve your significant other if you have one. Your partner is a parent, too. He (or she) *wants* to help. He *should* help. He *needs* to help. I was so possessive of my baby—and so insanely anxious (see above)—that I wanted to do it all. I didn't even mind the sleep deprivation. But in the process, I was cheating my husband out of essential bonding time with his son. And eventually, I didn't want to do it *all* by myself anymore. Remember: You're a team, and there's strength in numbers.

Premade meals will be your best friend. I love to cook, but it is nearly impossible to find the time to whip up anything in the kitchen in the first few weeks. How much time can it take to care for one tiny human? A LOT. And that tiny human always wants you when you're in the middle of something else— like attempting to chop vegetables or making sure the fish doesn't burn. Prepared meals from Fresh Direct, Blue Apron or Munchery, to name a few, are lifesavers. And down the road, if you're in the market for a gift for a new-mom friend, a gift certificate to one of these places is an easy and fantastic idea.

Buy yourself some sensible but stylish(ish) slip-on shoes. It was quite the rude awakening when my closetful of gorgeous shoes were now impractical…and the only truly comfortable shoes that I had were sneakers. I looked like a soccer mom way before my kid was able to play soccer. Don't put this errand on the back burner. Go out and get yourself a supercomfy pair of flats or rubber-soled slip-ons. It will make you feel better about your appearance *and* help you look better in your clothes. Trust me when I say that can make a world of difference, especially on the particularly tough days.

It will take you forever to do every little thing— yes, forever. OK, maybe not *literally* forever, but it will certainly feel like it. Between feeding the baby, changing a poopy diaper, swapping a puked-upon outfit, dressing yourself while tending to a crying child and packing a diaper bag, it's impossible to do things quickly. (And this actually gets comical when you add a second child to the mix.) Readjust your thinking, build in a lot of extra time and be realistic, and you'll be good to go...in, like, two hours.

Devise a plan for your baby photos, and stick with it. Is this really "mommy maintenance," you may be wondering? If you don't want to drown in a sea of adorable digital pictures and lose your damn mind, YES. I have to admit, I've done a terrible job of this, and now my collection of nearly 40,000 kid photos is so overwhelming, it's starting to give me nightmares. But I'm going to sort through them soon—or so I keep promising myself—because otherwise the problem will just get worse. Do yourself a favor and figure out a good, affordable photo-printing solution before baby is born, buy some albums and stay on top of this issue. (FYI, in case you were wondering, I didn't exaggerate that 40K number. God help me.)

And while you're at it, write *everything* down. In those early days, you think you will remember the minutiae of baby's wonderful progress and adorable little quirks, and you do for a while. But life takes over, and so many things vie for those few remaining precious brain cells of yours. Get in the habit of writing down the little milestones and the sweet moments every day, and by the time your kid is saying the cutest (and darndest) things, you'll still be doing it and you won't miss a memory.

Just say no. You're a mom now, so get used to using that little two-letter word. Visitors right after baby's birth if you don't want them there? Say it with me: No. Cereal in a 4-week-old's bottle, because that's the way our parents did it a million years ago? Say it with me again: No. Anything that's annoying and opinionated and unsolicited? Once more and with feeling: NO. See? Easy.

The love feels like it will crush you. I was not prepared for that intense, overwhelming, all-consuming feeling, but you know what? It was actually a lovely surprise. That love is wonderful and terrifying and amazing and paralyzing. Sometimes I felt like I couldn't breathe from it all, so I just sat there, staring at my perfect little miracle. There's no way to really understand this until you've been through it, but when you get there, enjoy it. Every minute of it.

ABOUT THE AUTHOR

Dawn Yanek is the proud mother of two mind-bogglingly energetic children, as well as the mom behind Momsanity.com. In a former life, she was an on-air spokesperson who discussed entertainment news, fashion and pop culture on TV. These days, she talks about slightly less glamorous things but has a ton of fun doing it. Her writing on parenting has also been featured on The Huffington Post, What the Flicka?, Healthline, BonBon Break and Scary Mommy. For more original content from Dawn, check out momsanity.com and join her on Facebook.

ABOUT MOMSANITY.COM

Momsanity is a judgment-free zone for moms—
especially new moms—where they can find parenting
tips, tricks, truths and maybe a tirade or two. Our
philosophy: Your support system shouldn't be left up
to luck. Every mom should have one. One that's free
of judgey relatives. One that's not made up of strange,
anonymous posters on social media telling you that
you're irrevocably damaging your child if you don't
make your own soap. One that's made up of women
who you like—and who are on the same crazy
parenting ride that you are *right now*. After all, you
might be crazy...but you're not alone.

Join us at momsanity.com, and subscribe to our
newsletter!

Made in the USA
San Bernardino, CA
20 April 2017